Advanced Praise

Lutheran pastor Paul Johnson finds spiritual nourishment in the small and quiet things in life. He writes about the prairies of South Dakota and the hills of Minnesota, the satisfaction of walking with a companion in the early morning and the power of whispering. These simple pleasures and challenges, often set in his hometown, offer lessons in mystery and joy.

Each essay ponders something encountered in daily life – the inspiration that dawns while weeding a rock garden, the sign in front of the local Baptist church that causes him to speculate that possibly God not only wants us to read the Bible but might also like for us to read novels, poetry and humor, too.

Read these short devotional pieces, many about the solace of nature, for pleasure and inspiration. These gentle meditations remind us that, indeed, God does work in mysterious ways.

Margaret Hawkins

Margaret Hawkins a writer and teacher. She is the author of *Lydia's Party*, *How We Got Barb Back*, and other books, as well as many articles and essays.

It has been my privilege and pleasure to receive the regular newsletter from Pastor Paul's parish. I have found his articles to be very readable, interesting, and a blessing.

In his writing Pastor Paul is a good teacher providing some excellent lessons. He asks good questions and answers them very well. He uses humor, wit, subtlety, and everyday experience. (He shares Scripture and an occasional quote from a book.) He sets forth simple lessons and serious thoughts about life, and best of all, he shares a clear Gospel of Jesus Christ. Thanks be to God for his ministry of writing.

Pastor Arvin Halvorson

I am able to relate to Pastor Paul's thoughtful reflections. His insights encourage me to continually look for God's presence all around me in daily life.

Rona Ford Johnson

A Walk with God
Discovering God in the Ordinary

Pastor Paul R. Johnson

Introduction

This collection of writings was originally part of my monthly and subsequently bimonthly church newsletters over the course of many years. With the help of friends who had found these writings helpful in their own journey of faith, together we chose these particular stories and essays.

Each essay or story relates to one of nature's four seasons—or one of the church's six seasons: Advent, Christmas, Epiphany, Lent, Easter, and Sundays after Pentecost—or even one of life's many seasons.

I hope you enjoy the journey this book offers to you.

A Walk with God
Discovering God in the Ordinary

Pastor Paul R. Johnson

A Walk with God: Discovering God in the Ordinary.
© Copyright 2020 Pastor Paul R. Johnson

All rights reserved. No part of this book may be used or reproduced in any manner whatsoever without written permission of the author except in the case of brief quotations embodied in critical articles and reviews.

The information in this book is distributed as an "as is" basis, without warranty. Although every precaution has been taken in the preparation of this work, neither the author nor the publisher shall have any liability to any person or entity with respect to any loss or damage caused or alleged to be caused directly or indirectly by the information contained in this book.

Printed in the United States of America

ISBN: 978-1-946195-81-4

Library of Congress Control Number: 2020917536

All Bible verse references are from the New Revised Standard Version Bible

Cover Design & Interior Book Design: Ann Aubitz

Published by FuzionPress
1250 E 115th Street,
Burnsville, MN 55337

A Word of Thanks

I thank the Good Lord for inspiration
and the right words at the right time.
I also wish to thank my family and friends
who helped and encouraged me in the adventure
of putting this collection of writings together.

A special thank you to the staff at Fuzion Press
and my editor, Connie Anderson,
for her insightful suggestions.
Together they made this adventure a reality.

Soli Deo Gloria
(Glory to God alone)

TABLE OF CONTENTS

STORY	MONTH	PAGE
1	March – April	11
2	May – June	13
3	May – June	15
4	November – December	17
5	September – October	19
6	September – October	22
7	May	24
8	May – June	26
9	November	29
10	January – February	31
11	January – February	34
12	March – April	36
13	March – April	38
14	June	40
15	May – June	42
16	March – April	45
17	March	47
18	May – June	49
19	May – June	51
20	March	52
21	March – April	54
22	May	56

23	June	59
24	September – October	61
25	January	63
26	September	65
27	September – October	67
28	July	69
29	June – August	71
30	November – December	73
31	November	75
32	June	78
33	July – August	80
34	January	82
35	December	84
36	December	86
37	December	88
38	August	90
39	January	92
40	July – August	94
41	August	96
42	July – August	98
	About the Author	100

1

MARCH – APRIL

Writing this month's message, I realize that both the Lenten and Easter seasons will occur during the timeframe of this newsletter. A picture comes to mind as I think about that. It is a view of the great and vast expanse of prairie in central South Dakota where we first lived. On afternoon drives in the country, it was inevitable that we would drive up a few of the small or not-so-small rises or hills. From there, we could see what seemed like "forever" stretched out before us. It was as though we saw not only our present location, but a future destination, as well as everything in between.

After spending some time enjoying the view, and marveling at the vastness of the prairie and sky, it was time to descend once again to venture either toward the destination or for home. In that sense, we always moved forward—obviously, since moving in reverse would be rather silly—to reach our goal and enjoy the past experience of the drive. We also looked forward to what lay ahead and encountering whatever it might be in between.

For you who are reading this, it is a similar experience. Next week we begin the Lenten season with Ash Wednesday. It is a season to reflect on the life of Jesus and the life of faith. It is a time to reflect on our lives with Jesus and to confess our shortcomings and sins that lie so close to us. Lent is a time to look forward as well to that final destination, that goal at the end of our journey that we call Easter.

Lent is made up largely of that "in-between" time when we encounter other experiences along the way during our life, and our time together in worship. For us, in our parish, we will encounter Luther's Small Catechism during our journey from Ash Wednesday to Easter Sunday. We will view each part of that book as a way to better understand the gifts and the life of faith that God gives to us and calls us to follow. As we move forward into this season, this journey, we can be thankful and appreciative of the treasure of the past that Luther gives to us in his writing from over 400 years ago.

And we can be thankful and expectant in the Easter season as we continue to move forward in faith and in life knowing that Jesus will be with us on this journey and will welcome us home. Knowing "the end" of the story, and where we are headed, means that the journey, the adventure isn't over. There is always something new to look forward to, and Jesus is always out ahead of us, calling us to follow him—and come what may, He will be with us just as He promises.

May you have a blessed Lenten and Easter season and journey.

2

MAY – JUNE

"We are a pilgrim people," a bishop once remarked. What is a "pilgrim people"? They are people on the go, on the move, and they don't necessarily have a place to call home. The writer to the Hebrews 11:13-14 echoes that statement, "All these (ancestors of faith) died without having received the promises, but from a distance saw and greeted them. They confessed that they were strangers and foreigners on the earth, for people who speak in this way make it clear that they are seeking a homeland."

As we transition from winter to spring, I am reminded of the truth of the text from Hebrews. There is something about the changes in the seasons that remind me, "I am a pilgrim, a foreigner, a stranger on the earth." Why? I don't really know why or how, it's just a feeling. Maybe it's the fact that in each season there is change, and something grows, something dies, something comes, and something goes.

"We are a pilgrim people." Perhaps one could also say we are a restless people—being "at home," yet not at home, being in the world, yet not of the world. Desiring a home, we look, we search, we create, we plan for a place, a time when we can settle down comfortably into life and live, yet knowing that there is a thin line between plans and life, between life and death, health and illness, and riches and poverty.

Maybe it's the "Northern Nordic Melancholia" that courses through my veins, but I find that in this season of transitions,

I, too, am restless and share the sentiment of Hebrews. The eruption of color, the sometimes-frosty mornings and warm afternoons, the bright skies, and lengthening days are all signs of a "restless" or season in transition looking and searching for its place, its home, and its time to be fulfilled.

But even in the transition or restlessness, there comes a peace that passes all understanding. With time, God's time, this same restlessness points me to God, His Word and promises. Only then, can I with the Psalmist cling to the promise in Psalm 46:1-2 . "God is our refuge and strength, a very present help in trouble…we will not fear, though the earth should change… ." I also call to mind the promise in Hebrews 13:8, "Jesus Christ is the same yesterday and today and forever."

"We are a pilgrim people"—yes, we are. Yes, we are strangers and foreigners on this earth, and we are sometimes restless. God always calls us to follow him, to find our homes, our places of rest and peace in Him and in His Word. Indeed, God never rests until He finds us. When we are found, God gives us His peace and rest, and we find that we are at home in Him.

Have a blessed spring along with all the other seasons that come and go, resting in the peace of God that surpasses all understanding.

3

MAY – JUNE

It's no secret that life changes. It is no secret that life has its challenges in store for us. With that said, I have become reacquainted with an old friend, the habit that I set aside for some time—the practice of walking. With that renewed friendship/practice, it set me to thinking and remembering.

In the Bible, it says that "…Noah walked with God" (Genesis 6:9). Even in the Garden of Eden, God walked to be with Adam and Eve (Genesis 3:8). There is something about walking that must be holy. I remember my own stories of walking. Years ago, there were walks in the still night air with friends, laughing and pondering the mysteries of life. Under the sparkling stars our friendship grew and deepened as we explored one street, then another.

We had walks in the countryside in the early morning hours. While people slept or farmers gathered their cows, we walked the roads, taking in the beauty of summer greenery, feeling the freshness of a new day with the dew still on the grass. The sweet aroma of fresh-cut hay drifted out over the pastures, filling our senses with life and peace.

Even into college and seminary, the walks included new friends, and were punctuated with laughter, and deep thoughts along a river path, city streets, or playgrounds. Each walk always seemed to be holy times, times to slow down, consider life and relationships, and God. It was on such a walk that I met my life partner. In the early morning hours before class, we walked and talked, learning to get to know each other, learning to hear and listen to one another's voice, and maybe even each other's hearts.

The walks have continued over the years through mountain grandeur, endless prairies, and wooded hills and valleys splashed with brilliant colors of wildflowers, like a bride dressed in her best. Walks have been taken with my children on the bike trail under the canopy of newly budded green branches with trees waking up after a long cold winter. Yes, even walks in the coldest winter, as the snow crunched, crackled, and creaked underfoot.

Which walk was most memorable? That would be hard to say. The answer may be, "all those that were shared with someone." Somehow those stand out above all the rest. Sharing a walk, a time with another person, is like no other experience.

Life is meant to be lived in relation to someone else. We are not created, nor is life created to be lived alone or in isolation. God walked with Adam and Eve. Noah walked with God, and so did Enoch and many others.

Of all the activities we have in life, walking is so simple, so plain, so ordinary and yet so blessed. It's brimming with promise and life, and is a God-given richness. May you, may we, make the time to walk not only with friends and family but also with God. You'll be glad you did.

4

NOVEMBER – DECEMBER

With Thanksgiving approaching in November and Christmas barely a month later in December, most of us will be preparing our homes for company and loved ones to gather. Many of our thoughts will be focused on what food we shall prepare for the holiday season. Invitations of one sort or another will be sent out to family, friends, and relatives, extending a warm welcome for their arrival at the celebrations and gathering of loved ones. With eager anticipation, we look forward to being surrounded by those closest to us.

While we may be planning and giving thanks for the many dishes of delicious entrées, desserts, and other delicacies, we know there are many other blessings to remember, such as home and family, work, good communities, to name a few. The blessings bestowed on us are many and varied. May God be praised for all His blessings.

But there is an aspect of the holiday season that we might overlook, quite unintentionally. That is, for some the holidays are not something to look forward to, because there will be an empty space around the table this year that wasn't there last year. Empty chairs and spaces in our lives and homes are all around us. They are simple and yet profoundly moving reminders that life is not always the same.

When we gather for the celebrations of Thanksgiving and Christmas, there may be empty spaces or chairs, place settings set out of habit for people who are loved but are no longer with us. Their absence is painfully noted and felt by all as the tears well up.

Have you ever wondered if God weeps as well when He sees empty chairs or spaces in our homes as we gather for feasts and celebrations? It may be a little hard to imagine God weeping, for who comforts God? When God prepares a feast for His children, sets the table, puts out the best dishes, and says, "come and eat, the feast is ready," what does God see and experience when there is an empty chair? Perhaps God does what Jesus did at the tomb of His friend Lazarus, and there was an empty space in His friend's home, Jesus wept.

And yet, even in His weeping, Jesus never forgot to give thanks to His heavenly Father for all things. In giving thanks, Jesus was filled with the peace of God that passed all understanding and kept His spirit strong in faith.

May you have a blessed holiday season, knowing that God is with you, blessing you with good things and notices and knows the empty places around the table and gathering of family, friends, and relatives.

5

SEPTEMBER – OCTOBER

What time are we living in? I am not asking which time zone or which year, and most of the time, I have a vague idea what time of day it is. What are the times we are currently living in, do you suppose?

The other reason I ask is because fall is approaching with all the programs and other events of school, church, and whatnot beginning again. My question also results from conversations I have now and then surrounding a variety of topics. What do you think, "What time are we living in?"

I am reminded of a famous quote from a book Charles Dickens published in 1859 titled *The Tale of Two Cities*. The opening line is, "It was the best of times, it was the worst of times...." I have heard that expression or a variation of that used to describe our time, whether it be society at large or even the Christian church (not any specific denomination).

A variation would be, "It is an exciting time to be the church." Related to the church would be articles and opinions that the present time is a time of great potential and possibilities relating to all the advances in medical and communication technologies, social media, and developments in the economic and political spheres of life, to name a few. I have also heard opinions that warn of the dangers of our times and what is wrong with our times.

I wonder then, which time it is, "the best or the worst?" I'm not sure I can speak for society for that's a bit overwhelming to ponder. I'm more familiar with the church, though still a "big" subject, and can offer something to think about. People have lived with this question or predicament for centuries. Perhaps the best answer is, "We live in both the best and the worst and always have." In the book of Esther, times were not good for the Jews, but Esther came into the king's service, and as her uncle, Mordecai told Esther, "Who knows? Perhaps you have come to royal dignity for just such a time as this" (Esther 4:14). With Esther as queen, it was the best of times. The book of Ecclesiastes states, "Do not say, "Why were the former days better than these?" (7:10).

From this observation, it seems the times are what they are, and we will experience both the best and the worst in any given age. However, that doesn't mean fate reigns supreme without any hope of things being different. Queen Esther found that out. She learned through her uncle Mordecai that "perhaps she has become Queen in this place, at this time for the reason that God can use for good" (to paraphrase the verse). The same is true today.

The question is universal and the response is equally universal and true for every age and time.

Whether the times are the best or the worst, they are certainly challenging both for society and the church. It is true that these are the best of times, and it is equally true that these are not the best of times (to put it differently). It also remains true that you and I are "brought here (or born) for just such a time as this." We are here for a reason. We have opportunities each day for good and for ill, for the best or the worst. God will work out His will for the world one way or another, with us or without us, as Mordecai also told Esther. But Esther could be part of God's work in that place and in that time.

Maybe the question is not "Are these times the best or the worst of times," but rather, "What can I do in these times for good, for what am I brought here in this place, at this time to do for good?" God is still at work creating order out of chaos, beauty out darkness, life out of death, and He still calls you and me to follow His Word "for just such a time as this."

Thank you for hearing the call of God and doing what you do for the Kingdom of God among us.

6

SEPTEMBER – OCTOBER

This is the time of year when things get a little goofy. I say that because we start to wonder, "Where did the summer go?" Maybe we had plans to do great things, fun things, exciting adventures and the like. Soon we are looking at the end of summer, and yet it feels like summer just started not that long ago. Maybe it's an age thing or maybe it's something else. Maybe it's just plain goofiness.

Or perhaps the sunspots are acting up and sending out rays that mess up our thinking and reasoning abilities. I read some time ago that this could be when time seems to sail right by us so quickly. But then again I am not so sure about that. Why would sunspots cause time to fly by, and affect me at the same time?

I feel perfectly fine. One day I asked a friend, "How are you today? Do you feel okay?" He said, "Yes, I am just great, and how are you?" "Well," I said, "I think I am fine, but something is a bit goofy lately. I can't explain it." My friend responded, "Now that I say that, you are right. I might as well confess that I too am feeling kind of dizzy these days. Let us work on this together and see if we can't do something about it." I was so glad when he said that. We agreed to meet again sometime soon to see what we could do about our problem.

Luckily for me we didn't have to meet like we planned. I went to a sale later that week and talked to another friend of mine and slowly I started feeling better. The dizziness started to subside and my thinking became clearer. I was so happy.

Well, so it goes. If this time of year starts to get you down because you didn't get everything done you had on your list, don't let it worry you. It's normal, it's not an age thing (mostly true), it's just being human. Always remember that even if time flies by too quickly and it will, God always has time for you and me. God always gives us time, whatever time that may be, as a gift of grace. There is always time to be grateful for the gifts that God has showered upon us. Isn't it a great gift to know that the Son of God shines upon us and can raise us to life and a new beginning each and every day?

May God bless your remaining summer days. Savor every day and look forward to the days and seasons ahead.

7

MAY

Nearby is a steepled white country church with an altar painting worth seeing. It is a painting of the invitation of the two men, on their walk to Emmaus, to Jesus to stay with them. Better yet, this invitation is in Norwegian. Unfortunately, it is usually blocked from view. Also, unfortunately, we do not read this text very often, and it is indeed a grand text. I like this story, and the painting brings the story to life. This painting can speak to us today about our walk of faith as the walk to Emmaus changed the lives and faith of Cleopas and his friend.

These two men walked along a dusty road, and while they walked, they visited, discussed, pondered, and wondered about the deep and tragic events that had just taken place in Jerusalem.

This reminds me of the many walks I used to take with friends years ago. Along the way, we would discuss many of life's challenges, joys, frustrations, and questions. During those walks, we also gave each other encouragement as we shared our burdens. Looking back on those walks, they were indeed a blessed time.

As the men approached Emmaus, Jesus joined them. Although they didn't recognize Him because of their grief, Jesus entered into their discussion and added to it by explaining the scriptures to them. As they later discovered, their hearts felt strangely warmed or on fire while Jesus spoke to them. Perhaps that helps to explain their invitation to Jesus to stay with them. They felt an inexplicable desire for Jesus to stay with them as

He offered himself to them in their conversation, discussion, and finally, in the breaking of bread. In an act that resembles worship, the breaking of bread, Jesus is revealed to them and their eyes were opened. In that act of breaking bread together with Jesus in their grief, the reality of the resurrection became real and their lives were changed.

In much the same way, we as a church, find ourselves walking on the road to Emmaus. We walk with friends, neighbors, colleagues, and fellow members discussing the events that have taken place in recent history. We speak of other challenges facing the church, families, communities, and even the nation. As we walk, we wonder what will or might happen. We wonder because we believe that the church is the place where we can find that certain something for our souls, spirits, hearts, and minds that brings peace, certainty, and hope. Into this discussion comes Jesus, and sometimes we do not recognize Him because our eyes are clouded. As we continue our journey of faith with fellow believers, we extend the invitation, more of a prayer that Jesus would come in and stay with us. We need to be in the presence of the risen Lord.

His presence among us becomes clearer when we worship together and we break bread together. It is in the act of worship that our eyes can be opened, and we see the risen Lord among us. It is in worship, in the hearing of the Word, the prayers, the songs of praise and the sacraments that Jesus comes to us and our eyes of faith are opened and we can say, "Were not our hearts burning as the Word was spoken and the bread of life broken and shared with us?" Never underestimate the power of worship with others and our walk of faith together. Jesus will meet us on the road and in our worship, and we will be changed.

Have a blessed Easter season (it isn't over with yet).

The walk to Emmaus story is found in Luke 24:13-35.

8

MAY – JUNE

The beauty and joy of our Easter worship is still vivid and fresh as I write this, and as you read this. In fact, the aroma of the lilies and other flowers lingers still in the church. The grass is greening, the buds are popping, and leaves unfold on the trees. Tulips, daffodils, and other flowers push their way up through the ground, filling us with eager anticipation for new life and a splash of bright colors. The morning dawns with light and hope as the birds welcome the sun. What the Psalmist wrote so long ago is certainly true, "This is the day that the Lord has made, let us be glad and rejoice in it" (Psalm 118:24).

It is also in this spirit of thanksgiving and anticipation that we celebrated Rogation Sunday recently. That was a day to give thanks to God for crops, fields, laborers who work the fields, and anticipation for a bountiful harvest. As our hearts, minds, hands, and thoughts turn to one of our basic human traits of growing things from the ground, consider the following spiritual garden of the heart and soul we can all plant.

For a garden of the heart and spirit we need vegetables for we are by nature vegetarians to a degree (read Genesis chapter 1). Plant a few rows of peas: Preparedness, Perseverance, Politeness, Patience, Prayer, and Praise. Then follow that with some lettuce: let us be truthful, let us be loyal, let us work together, let us worship, let us be thankful, and let us be joyful.

What vegetable garden would be complete without squash? Plant a few rows of squash, squash gossip, squash indifference, squash ingratitude, and spaghetti squash (I know that doesn't quite fit our "spiritual garden," but it sounds fun.)

If you are into turnips, how about the following varieties of turnips: turn up with a smile, turn up with a new idea, turn up with determination, turn up with a friend or neighbor at worship or a special church event and turn up with a heart full of joy.

Of course, carrots are also good for us to eat as well. When you "care at all," you naturally give thanks to God for all your daily blessings, are happy for your friends and neighbors good fortune in life, do what you are able to for the betterment of our community and our churches.

That should give us a good start for a garden of the heart and soul.

I also noticed that God gave Adam and Eve the fruit of the trees to eat. Maybe we're a bit fruity, too. Try planting some apple trees. Tell someone they are the "apple of your eye" and see what happens. Or I suppose you could tell your Granny Smith that you would like a Macintosh for a big Gala that you are planning. Wouldn't' it be fun to plant a banana tree and go "bananas" with opportunities for Bible Study, volunteerism in the community or church? Be careful though if you plant berries, because "life is the berries" sometimes. Be wary of chokecherries. The same would be true of cherries, and peaches. These might remind us that life can be "the pits," although life can be "peachy" too. Whatever fruit you plant, pray that the fruits of the Spirit will produce a bountiful harvest: love, joy, peace, patience, kindness, goodness, faithfulness, gentleness, and self-control.

I think I better quit before this gets too corny. Whatever garden you chose to plant in your soul and life, be sure to water it well with prayer, God's Word and the light from His Son. It will be sure to grow and produce a bountiful harvest.

Have a blessed summer.

9

NOVEMBER

Tis the season to be... I guess that's the wrong season. It's still too early for that one. But it will soon be the season to give thanks for all the blessings of life. Thankfully, this particular season, sandwiched between two more profitable seasons, isn't saturated with commercialism.

Just thinking about the tables laden with bowls of food, hot, steaming, and dripping with butter and gravy, causes reactions similar to Pavlov and his experiments. From somewhere out of the blue comes a most curious phrase, bringing some interesting pictures to mind. The phrase is… "You are what you eat." What happens if we change that just a bit to state, "You eat what you are?" You might agree that some pretty silly images come to mind when thinking about Thanksgiving and what it is that we love to prepare and eat.

I'd be a real turkey if I didn't think there was some truth in that statement. Again, it might just all be a bunch of baloney, and I'd be accused of being a fruit cake or at best bananas. The more I think about that phrase and thanksgiving, the harder it is to squash it. I am reminded that if I don't mind my P's (peas) and Q's, people will believe that I am corny and probably won't think I'm worth a hill of beans to listen to.

It is at times like this I need to talk to my peach of a pumpkin or sweetie pie as she prepares yet another dish of vegetables. Seeing how I am such a ham at times, she patiently listens, wondering if I'd hit the sauce a bit, and if I had, that would certainly take the cake and be the berries as we are expecting a dinner table packed with guests like sardines in a can. With all the preparations needed for the big day, I guess I can't afford to be a couch potato and had better beef up my culinary skills of carving whatever dish will be served.

But after all is said, prepared, baked, cooked, steamed, and done, it is good to look forward to the time when we all gather around the table, bow our heads and say, "Lettuce pray... ."

P.S. As you look forward to the great feast of Thanksgiving, and the anticipation of celebrating it with those you love, don't forget to also fill your soul, heart, and mind with the nourishment of spiritual food that comes from the smorgasbord of God's Word, worship, devotions, prayer, songs, and meditative silence. Remember, "You are what you eat" and "You eat what you are."

You and I are children of God, and we have spirits that need spiritual food. In the season of thanksgiving, it is good to say, "Let us pray...thank you Father for....fill us with your Spirit that we may... ."

Have a blessed Thanksgiving. As a spiritual appetizer, consider reading Philippians 4:4-9.

10

JANUARY – FEBRUARY

Merry Christmas! It should still be the Christmas season when you read this. Don't forget that the Christmas season lasts 12 days after Christmas day, and ends on January 5, the day before Epiphany. There is a reason for the Christmas carol reflecting those 12 days. Technically, Christmas is a rather short season; Advent is much longer. It's too bad that in many places and situations, for many people, Christmas is about over after supper on the 25th of December. That's when Christmas is just beginning!

But for all that, this whole season is truly wonderful. The colors, the aromas of baking, sweets, evergreens, twinkling lights, glitter, shiny tinsel, boxes, ribbons, and bows, all make for a wonder-filled time with friends and family alike. Like most good things in life, Advent/Christmas speeds by far too fast. Before we know it, we're back to the usual routine in January, and it is cold, dark, and rather bland looking outside without all the decorations. Maybe that's why I simply left our lights up all year last time around. I didn't always light them, but since our lights are red, white, and blue, not only do they represent Christmas, but I can light them up for a few other holidays as well.

Oh, we also keep a few nativity scenes up all year in our home to remind us that Jesus is born for us, and that in a very real sense, Christmas is a year-round celebration as Jesus comes to us each and every day. In the past few years another event has endeared itself to me about Christmas. For that reason, I look forward to Christmas every year in another way. What might that event be? In the days just before Christmas, the days start getting longer and the nights shorter.

The winter solstice (usually around December 21 or 22) begins the change in the lightness of each day. I am reminded of the words of St. John, "The light shines in the darkness and the darkness did not overcome it" (John 1:5). The light of Jesus' life and His life-giving words are as light in the darkness of sin, and all that sin brings to our world. It's a funny thing about this solstice, but even though the days begin to get longer, the temperature usually gets colder, and winter becomes rather "bitter," difficult and something to endure. What is wonderful about the solstice is that it is a clear and definitive sign that winter will not last forever, the darkness will not last indefinitely. The winter solstice and Christmas time both are filled with hope, and we are looking forward to brighter days.

That is also why we celebrate the birth of Jesus, whether it is in December or July. But, what a wonderful time to celebrate the light of God's love, life, forgiveness, grace, mercy, and all the other gifts He has to give us than this time of year as the darkness gives way to the light. Yes, the saying is true: *Jesus is the reason for the season.* Jesus is for all seasons, and in Jesus there is always light and life. When I think of winter in this way, it's not so bad after all, because the days are getting longer and the light is shining brighter day by day.

May your New Year be as bright as the lengthening days and blessed abundantly by the God of light.

11

JANUARY – FEBRUARY

The stockings had all been hung with care in the hopes for Santa to visit. The tree had been decorated with care and excitement in eager anticipation of finding just the right gift under its brightly colored ornaments and lights. The nativity had been unpacked with reverence and awe as wistful memories of Christmases gone by replayed their joys once again. It was a good Christmas celebration.

Now the time has come once again to put away all the ribbons, bows, boxes, tinsel, lights, ornaments, wreaths and yes, take down the tree. That may be the hardest one to put away. Without the tree, the "spirit" of Christmas seems to dissipate, and the ordinariness of the daily routine of life in mid-winter returns. (We live in Minnesota, and there's a reason we have a hymn titled, "In the Bleak Midwinter.")

Is it possible to preserve some of the beauty, hope, color, and anticipation of Christmas at least until late winter or early spring?

Yes, perhaps there is a way to do that, but it is not an easy thing to do. What is that way? It is to remember the words of the angel to the shepherds on that dark night of the first Christmas, "Do not be afraid…I am bringing good news; to you is born this day a Savior…" (Luke 2:10-11). When we return to the joys and challenges of our daily routines, remember the words "Do not be afraid…to you is born a Savior," using your name after the words "to you." Those few words are a central message throughout scripture. Also, remember the name of Jesus that St. Matthew writes of when he quotes the prophet Isaiah, "Look, the virgin shall conceive and bear a son, and they shall name Him Emmanuel which means, "God is with us" (Matthew 1:22-23).

These too, are good words to remember. "Emmanuel, God is with us." God is with us in our winters, springs, summers, and autumns. God is with us in our hopes and dreams. God is with us in our joys, sorrows, celebrations, and heartaches. God is with us in our giving and receiving, our good days and our bad days.

To aid us in remembering, try leaving out a small nativity set to "see and hear" once again the words of the angel and the prophet about the child who is born for you and me... "Do not be afraid. I am bringing good news, to you is born a Savior. And His name is Emmanuel."

It's all right to leave up a nativity set year around because if it's true that every Sunday is a celebration of Christ's resurrection, every day is a day to celebrate His name: "Emmanuel—God with us."

May you have a blessed and peace filled New Year. *God is with you.*

12

MARCH – APRIL

I don't know about you, but I think the timing of the Lenten season this year was absolutely fantastic and rich with meaning and even humor. If nothing else, the dates for Ash Wednesday and Easter should cause an eyebrow to raise, and a look of wonderment come across our faces.

What might it mean for us in this year of 2018 that Ash Wednesday occurred on Valentine's Day? Isn't Valentine's Day a day to celebrate love and warm fuzzy feelings? Isn't Ash Wednesday a rather somber day to confess our sins and remember the sacrifice of Jesus on the cross? Well…yes, but what we read in John 3:16 is also true.

"For God so loved the world that He gave His only Son…" We could say that Valentine's Day, when celebrated in our world of faith, is simply another expression of God's great love for us. Jesus is God's greatest Valentine's Day gift and wish for us. That puts a different perspective on both Ash Wednesday and Valentine's Day, doesn't it?

This timing thing only gets better with Easter. Of all the days that Easter can fall on in the spring, this year it falls on April Fool's Day. Can it get any better than that? The last time it happened was 1956. The next time will be in 2029, and the last time for this century that April Fool's and Easter are the same day will be 2040.

April Fool's Day is when we love to trick people with words and pranks. April Fool's Day might be a day to be on your guard in case something unexpected happens. Well, Easter certainly fits the bill for April Fool's Day. St. Luke writes in his gospel as the women come back to tell the disciples that Jesus had risen from the dead, "but these words seemed to them (the disciples) an idle tale and they did not believe the women" (Luke 24:11). I wonder if St. Luke left out a comment or thought on the part of the disciples, such as "Jesus is alive? Are you telling us a joke? We aren't fools you know."

On the other hand, Easter is a pretty good joke for God to play on Satan. I imagine Satan figured he had silenced Jesus once and for all. Easter wasn't in his plans. In a very real sense, God has the last word, and also the last laugh on Satan with the resurrection of Jesus.

It is for this reason that I believe April Fool's Day is an appropriate and even the best day to celebrate Easter. The message of Easter is certainly not easily believed, and sounds incredulous and unbelievable. But in faith, we do believe Easter is true. We believe that there is life again. We believe what common sense and the experiences of everyday life would not have us believe. We believe that God in His love for the world and us chose to give life again to Jesus, because of God's great love for the world, which in light of what happened to Jesus would seem a rather foolish expression of God's love.

But isn't that what love is all about? Isn't love itself rather foolish? People in love certainly do foolish things sometimes. Loving another person who has faults, failures, weaknesses, vulnerabilities, shortcomings, and all the rest, isn't that a foolish thing to do and to even believe is possible? Thank goodness people sometimes believe what they do not see. Thank goodness, better yet thank God, that people love others as they do. Where would we be without the foolishness of love?

When we believe that Easter is true, we also believe that love conquers evil, hopelessness, despair, and things like that. Easter may be God's last laugh on Satan, but Easter is our foundation of hope that each day is worth living for. Easter is God's "yes" to life.

When April Fool's Day arrives, be sure to say a prayer of thanksgiving for God's gift of love and what might appear as foolishness. God's foolishness is our salvation and the hope for the world.

13

MARCH – APRIL

Soon it will be the Easter season, and we will hear the glorious news that Jesus is risen from the dead! He is alive. Death no longer has power over us. It's great and marvelous news, something everyone should hear and know.

We have a message to proclaim to a world where it seems people flit here and there and everywhere in an effort to find life. In a society that seeks unconditional love and compassion, and a commitment of heart and soul that will last beyond the whims of our fickle and rollercoaster emotions, we have a message that fulfills such longings. Will anyone hear us?

I ask the question because on Easter Sunday, our usual response is to shout out the good news. That's a good practice while we are in church, but will the rest of the world stop to listen? Will shouting get the message across? I wonder.

There's already so much noise around. Finding a place where we aren't bombarded with noise is nearly impossible. It's easier for us to tune something or someone out if it seems they are the least bit noisy. So what about our Easter message?

I have an idea. Maybe we should whisper the message to people. Have you ever noticed that whispering can generate a lot of attention? Have you ever started whispering to someone only to have others stop and try to listen to what you were saying? I don't mean by whispering that we should not tell the message or be timid about it. The message *has* to be told—it *needs* to be told. However, if we want people's attention, maybe they'd listen more if we whispered.

There is one advantage to whispering over shouting. When you whisper, you have to be close to someone. Shouting can be directed at anyone or no one in particular. We don't really need more impersonal interactions with people in this world. Whispering on the other hand always directs itself to at least one person in particular. Isn't that the whole point of sharing the Good News? What better way to show one person at a time that the message is "for them," than to whisper that it is just for them?

Come to think of it, what do you suppose our world would be like if more people whispered? There are already enough people shouting who want to be heard for one reason or another, for both good and bad reasons at that.

Maybe if we whispered, we would hear God too. God's mode of communication is not only through a loud booming voice or a choir of legions of angels. Consider Elijah, the great Old Testament prophet, who did not hear God in the great strong wind, nor earthquake, nor in the fire, but only in the "still small voice" (1 Kings 19:11-12).

Sometimes there is nothing louder than silence. *Think about that one for a while.* Sometimes the best way to be heard is to whisper. We have great news, freeing news, life-giving news—how shall we proclaim it so people will hear and hopefully listen?

14

JUNE

God's will. She had often thought about that subject over the years. She had wondered about God's will many a time. What was God's will, had she followed God's ways? In her younger years, she thought she could usually discern God's will, but as she grew older, she wasn't always so sure. Some days she didn't have a clue about God's will. Now she thought about it again in a different sort of way as she sat in her living room recalling the times of her life.

Those years that have come and gone so quickly now seem like a dream. Wasn't it just yesterday she was a child playing with her mom and dad, running, jumping, and squealing with delight? And her teenage years, tumultuous as they were, were they not just a moment ago? Had she followed God's will, had she listened to God when she made the decisions she did back then?

As the clock on the wall ticked the minutes away in her small living room, filling the silence with a rhythmic sound, she reminisced on the years with her husbands. She had had two; the first one died at a young age. They had so many plans, hopes, and dreams. That was a hard time. Now her second husband's funeral was just a few days ago. What would she do now? What was God's will? Could anyone ever fill her life as her husbands had each in their own way? She wondered long and hard on that one.

Then she looked across the room at all the pictures of children and grandchildren lined neatly on the top of the television. She remembered all her questions and her prayers during those years. Had she raised her children right? Had she followed God's will, "What was God's will for her as a parent"? When she was young, she was certain of God's will. When her children grew and became more independent, she had her doubts. Being a parent was not easy. Being a parent was a struggle, yet she always prayed that she might do God's will, whatever it was.

God's will. As she sat in her chair, with hands folded on her lap, her eyes quietly moved their gaze from one object to another. She began to realize that she no longer wondered so much about what God's will was, so much as she was thankful that God had always been with her throughout the years. God had indeed been with her in her rebellious teenage years. God had been with her through the dark days of her first husband's death. God had been there to bring life and light again, opening her heart to love another husband again. God had been there as she raised a family. God had watched over her as she declined in health and the years advanced.

Rocking slowly, she closed her eyes and thought to herself, "Imagine that—God has always been with me, doing His will, and I am just noticing now, after all these years." Then she said a prayer, "Thank you Lord for your promises. Thank you for your faithfulness. You have always been with me, and you have always been at my side. Your will has been done. How can I ever thank you enough?"

When she finished, she rocked some more, basking in the peaceful knowledge that her years were and had been in the hands of a loving God, whose will was done and whose will it was that she, His child, might only believe His promises.

15

MAY – JUNE

I know this is the May-June newsletter, and that within these months, we will celebrate both Mother's Day and Father's Day. I am not able to do justice to both in one article. I ask that as you read this article, you would also remember the importance of fathers in our lives—and who has been a "father" figure, mentor, faith teacher or role model for you.

For this Mother's Day, I would like to share with you my thoughts about the church. In church history and tradition, the church has been personified by a woman. Revelation 19:7 poetically writes of the marriage of the Lamb (Jesus) and his bride. In Ephesians 5:27, St. Paul writes of the church as a wife who is blameless and holy. Some have even called the church, "the mother of our faith." With that, I'd like to introduce you to the church, the mother of my faith.

She is quite a lady. Her energy and vibrancy betray her age, and most of the time she puts me to shame with her vigor and zest for living.

Over the years I have grown to appreciate her friendship more and more. I suppose I could even describe our friendship as something much deeper than that. She first knew me when I was but a baby and she held me in her arms. She cradled me gently and spoke kind and gracious words in my ears. She was patient as I grew, patient even if I was rather rambunctious and loud in her house. She was with me when I first started learning, and she taught me many lessons about life and faith.

Even on the days I was more interested in talking than listening, she persevered and remained faithful in her tasks of teaching, listening, guiding, and befriending me.

When I was maturing into a young man, she was there, as always, inviting me to come and sit a spell and listen to her words, even as she listened to mine. When the days of doubt and darkness came and faith seemed to be distant and far away, she was still there, and she continued to invite and listen.

By her encouragement, she watched me enter the seminary to seek a life of faithful service to God. Through her loving ways, she blessed the new chapters of life as they came my way—marriage and family—and she offered wise counsel.

It was fortunate for me that she was able to be present at the birth of my children and as she did so many years before, she took those new lives in her hands, gently cradled them in her arms, and spoke to them of love and God's promises. Then she handed them back to me and said, "They are yours to guide, to love, and to teach all that I have taught you."

She has always been there for me. She is a grand lady, fit for a king. Even as life changes or when I walk through dark valleys or empty spaces, she is there with me, always inviting me to come and sit a spell and to listen, even as she listens to me. When days are bright and good, joyous, and overflowing with blessings, she is always there, inviting me to come and…

Now as I look her in the eye, I see something that maybe I haven't seen before. In her eyes is a depth of faith, love, and hope that knows no bounds. In her eyes sparkles the gift of life, and in her eyes there burns a compassion that knows the depths of sorrow and the heights of joy.

Yet in those same eyes I have seen something else of late. In her eyes there is the searching gaze of a mother seeking her children. She seeks them out, so that she can invite them to come and sit a spell to listen, even as she promises to listen to them. I wonder if those eyes will find who they are looking for. I sometimes wonder if her children will find her.

And so the years go on and her friendship grows with each passing year. Perhaps what makes her so wonderful is her timelessness and her agelessness. I am glad she took me in as a friend and a child of God so many years ago. I can never thank God enough for this friend He has given me.

Who is this friend, you might be wondering or asking—this friend fit for a king who is faithful and loving? Join me on Sunday mornings; we will sing, pray and listen together in her house, for there you will meet her.

16

MARCH – APRIL

Have you ever had the feeling that there are things in life that are so close you can feel them, but not quite fully? The same might be true when the feeling is expressed that you have a hunch, an intuitive realization about something, but can't quite put your finger on it? Something is real, but at the same time, it isn't yet a realized fact. Does this sound familiar? If so, then that is how the dates of this newsletter come to me.

I look out the window and I see winter. I walk out the door and I feel winter. I look at the calendar and I see spring is almost here, but not yet. I look at the newsletter and I see the months "March/April," and I feel the tension between winter and spring. I also experience both Lent and Easter all at the same time. We are currently in Lent, but Easter is close at hand, but not yet celebrated. Do we focus on what is remaining of Lent or do we look forward and concentrate on Easter and simply bypass Lent?

As far as the seasons go, I'd just as soon skip winter (that's an age thing) and get right to a long, beautiful, warm, pleasant life-awakening spring. However, when the cold and beauty of winter is acknowledged and appreciated, are not the gifts of spring even more celebrated, cherished, and loved?

There are signs of spring around us, occasional warm days, dormant buds on branches, and the calendar. Spring is not yet realized, but we can still rejoice that the promised warmth and beauty will soon be realized because the signs are present and the promise of new life can be trusted.

The same is true of our lives of faith and the promise of new life, forgiveness, and salvation. We live in the "in-betweenness" of life—death and new life... We live in the "now-but-not-yet"-ness of sin and righteousness.

We live in between the present reality of sin in the world and our lives (the cross or season of Lent/Good Friday), and the hope and reality of new life, new beginnings and the promise of forgiveness and life because of Jesus' resurrection to new life (empty tomb or season of Easter).

We can live in this in-betweenness because we believe that the resurrection and promise of new life is true. We can live in the "now" of winter with the joy of the "not-yet" spring because we know and believe that spring does, in fact, come. We can live in the realization that yes, there is sin and evil in the world, and it is awful, heart-wrenching, scary and uncertain, yet we can have hope, joy, and certainty that it will end someday because *love is more powerful than hate, life is stronger than death, light is stronger than darkness and God is trustworthy, true, faithful and full of life, light, and love.*

May God bless your seasons of life and the faith journey you are currently traveling. God is with you now, and will continue to be in what is yet to come.

17
MARCH

The seasons come and go. Although in Minnesota it seems that one season in particular gets more than its fair share of time in our lives. Maybe that's the reason we look forward to the other three seasons so much. It's nice to have some variety. It shouldn't surprise anyone that our mood and general demeanor are shaped and influenced by the seasons. With each season we dream about what we hope to accomplish and fulfill as plans are made and carried out. Sharing our thoughts, hopes, and dreams with one another, we also share encouraging words so the season may be rich and full for all.

So it is with the seasons of the church year. With each season, there is a different experience. We started with Advent, continued with Christmas, then Epiphany. Each season carries with it the anticipation of exciting events that fill our lives with light, color, beauty, words of love, hope, and peace.

We are about to enter another season. It is the season of Lent. Like Advent, Lent is a season of anticipation and preparation. We anticipate the joy of the resurrection of Jesus (simply because we are Easter people). We also need the time of preparation for the celebration of Easter. Lent offers us a time of reflection and meditation on the life of Jesus. Lent offers a time and opportunity to express our thanksgiving and humble gratitude for the life He lived among us and for us. Lent is a time to gather together for worship, prayer, hymns, and meditation on the Word, the story of Jesus.

This year we will ponder the meaning of the seven last words of Jesus from the cross. In and through these words we hear an amazing story of a profound and life-changing love. *There is no other story like this story.*

In this season of Lent and preparation for the good news of Easter, I offer you a hymn that will fit in with these words of Jesus from the cross. It is a wonderful hymn by Isaac Watts called, "When I Survey the Wondrous Cross." It is a simple hymn with no special story that highlights its origin or history. What makes it so profound and moving is the imagery of the words. Its power lies in its stark and truthful revelation of our sin and the suffering of Jesus on account of that sin. Its beauty is found in the picture it paints of the profound and immeasurable love of God in Jesus as He offers himself on the cross for the world, including you and me.

Take some time in this Lenten season to read and meditate on the words of this hymn, "When I Survey the Wondrous Cross." You might be able to find it in a hymn book—or even find it on-line.

May this season be a blessing to you.

18

MAY – JUNE

We have a music CD at home with songs created from various Bible stories. The lyrics to the lead song contain the words: "listen to your mother's words…." These words mirror the cover picture on the CD of a woman surrounded by many children who are listening to her reading the words of scripture.

It is a picture showing a truth worth seeing and remembering as Mother's Day approaches. It is also a good picture of the church, as the place where faith is given birth and is nurtured in the lives of all who belong to God's family of believers.

I am reminded of the story my own mother tells of when I was but a wee child who would sit on her lap. Every day at noon, I would run to her and jump into her lap to hear her tell me a story. I don't remember the stories anymore, but a bond between mother and son was formed, fashioned, and strengthened with each story time shared. Needless to say, that habit did not last long, but those times were priceless. I'm sure my mother didn't mind that I stopped as I didn't stay small very long, and she wouldn't have appreciated a big kid plopping into her lap.

Our faith is nurtured in our homes. Our faith is also nurtured in the church. The church is the place where families gather with others to hear the story of God's love and mighty deeds again, and to grow in their faith.

The church is often referred to as the bride of Christ. The church is, in one sense, the mother of our faith. Through the church—the people of God, not the building—we are nurtured in the faith that is planted in us by God's Holy Spirit in baptism. In the lap of the church, we hear God's Word, the story of God's love and forgiveness, and the story of Jesus, God's son. In the lap of the church, we can rest our weary souls and receive the embracing arms of love like those of our mothers.

As we grow in years, our relationship with the church may change, but the years of love, storytelling, welcoming, and sharing the Christian faith we had as infants and children, are always remembered and cherished.

But lest we leave out our fathers, as Father's Day is also approaching, let us not forget that the church also reflects the love and strong arms of fathers as they too live as examples of faithfulness and love for their children. The people of God gather together to support, encourage, and rejoice as children grow and mature, taking on the challenges and questions of life and faithfulness each and every day.

For Mother's Day in May and Father's Day in June, perhaps you can find a way to thank the mothers and fathers in your life that spent time with you, giving you and nurturing in you a faith that has grown through the years. If possible, find a way to thank your church, "our mothers and fathers of faith," the people of God who with God's help and Holy Spirit, nourished, supported, and encouraged your faith to grow and flourish.

19

MAY – JUNE

It is difficult to write an article about spring and the months of May and June when there is so much snow on the ground. By the time you read this, hopefully the snow will be gone, and the flowers will be coming up in the garden.

Yet, even with the snow blanketing the ground, the hope and allure of spring is strong, and we know with certainty that spring will come. We can be confident of the promise of new life, color, planting, gardens growing, and producing delights for our mealtimes, as well as all the other favorite pastimes that summer brings.

In this season of spring and new life, the ground soaks up the sun's warmth, and the gentle rains come. Now we long to soak up the warmth of the sun and feel its effect on us, invigorating us to action and the joys of summer.

What is true for the earth and our lives is also true for our souls. How often our souls long to soak up the light of God's Son and feel the showers of His blessings upon us.

As we anticipate and eagerly await spring and summer and the activity that these seasons offer, let us not forget to feed, nourish, water, and sustain our spirits with the Word of God. Wherever you find yourself this spring and summer, remember to pray and take a few minutes each day to read a portion of God's Word. You'll be glad you did.

We take care of our yards, gardens, and homes, let us do the same for our souls. Have a great summer.

20
MARCH

Have you ever had the experience of noticing something as though for the first time, yet knowing that it is obviously something you should have known for a long time? And when this happens you feel rather foolish. Well, this happened to me recently, and it was like the heavens opened, and heavenly music rang out in my ears, and my eyes were opened. I was sitting in my office, visiting with a member when I noticed that the clock showed that it was 5:15 pm. I thought, "Wow, it's still light out! The days are getting longer." Then I thought, "Duhhh…of course, the days are longer, it's been nearly two months since that started."

I suppose with all the snow, snow and more snow that we have received and is still piled high, we don't notice that the days are getting longer. The sun's power is getting stronger, and the few days when the ice and snow melt and settle more, all this gets forgotten. I don't notice what is right before my eyes—spring is getting closer all the time.

Slowly, imperceptibly at times, whether we notice it or not, the sun does get stronger, the snow and ice do begin to melt, the days do get longer, and the promise of spring draws nearer and nearer even without our asking or working for it. The hand of God simply works among us. God directs the course of the seasons, as well the sun, moon, and stars for He made them. God sends the rain to fall on the just and the unjust. God causes the sun to shine on the righteous and the sinner, the repentant, and the unrepentant.

God even makes the days longer in spite of my inability to notice or your ability to notice and be grateful. Isn't that grand? Isn't that good news?

I wonder if the same isn't true of the Kingdom of God and whether we notice it or not among us. Jesus said, **"Repent, for the kingdom of heaven has come near"** (Matthew 4:17). He also said in Luke 17:21 in response to the Pharisees, "The Kingdom of God is not coming with things that can be observed....For in fact, the Kingdom of God is among (within) you." The Kingdom is already here, have you noticed? The hands of God are working in, around and among us already. Slowly, imperceptibly, whether we notice it or not, God is with us and wherever God is, there is life, new life, and a new creation.

But there are days that, like the dark, cold winter nights, we fail to see what is happening around us, and still the Kingdom comes to us day by day. Then, by the grace of God, we have those precious moments when the heavens open, the heavenly music rings in our ears, and our eyes are opened, at least for a brief moment, and we see the hand of God among us. Perhaps we witness the baptism of a child in a new way. We hear the Word of God spoken as though for the first time, and our hearts are warmed. Perhaps the word and a hand of forgiveness are extended to us by one whom we have drifted away from.

As the Son begins to shine brighter and brighter, dispelling the darkness of sin from our lives, take time to notice the hand and work of God among us, and give God praise and thanksgiving as He brings the Kingdom to each person in our community and churches.

21

MARCH – APRIL

Easter is still six weeks away as I write this, and because it is a bi-monthly newsletter, the hope and promise of spring will also soon be upon us. Yet it's all hard to imagine as I look out the window at the winter wonderland of snow and frost. It is a beautiful scene to be sure, but it is not the picture of a colorful spring day filled with light and expectant new life budding and blooming among the trees and gardens in our yards. Even so, we plan, we hope, we dream, and we wait with eagerness for the new day. The seed catalogs come, and we envision our spring and summer gardens filled with vegetables, fruit, and other delicious things to eat. We plan and prepare ourselves for that time and season…and it is good.

So it is with our faith. Currently, we are on our Lenten journey of "facing the cross" and all that comes with it. It is not always a bright and cheerful picture, but we have hope and the promise of Christ's resurrection to look forward to. Just as we must go through winter before spring comes, we must experience the Lenten journey in our faith walk. In our faith, as in our lives, we plan, we hope, and we dream of what it means to be Easter people who have gone through the season of Lent. In this world of darkness, sin, and sometimes fear of what is to come of all this, it might be hard to see the Easter promise of life, so it is good to bring out the "catalog" book of life. It is good to see and do those things that keep our hearts, souls, and minds on Jesus and the many gifts and blessings He gives to us. It is good to prepare our hearts, souls, and minds for that Easter day filled with life, light, and love with scripture, worship, prayer, praise, thanksgiving, and fellowship.

Of course, the best part of spring garden planning is seeing the fruits of your labors, not to mention the tasting and eating of it too. Might it not be similar with the planning, preparing, and taking care of the garden of faith within our hearts, souls, and minds? Isn't it good to see and experience a few of the fruits of faith growing and producing good things in your life and in the lives of those who share that faith?

May God bless your preparations for Easter and the seasons of life that follow.

22
MAY

We made our annual family pilgrimage again this year to "do the graves." It was a beautiful, sunny, and fresh warm spring day. When we arrived at our destination, we noticed that nothing had changed, which was to be expected. Then we set about our business of planting flowers.

Walking among the grave markers I saw names I already knew and others that were becoming more familiar to me. As we approached the first ones, someone again told stories of the loved ones resting in that place as we planted the flowers.

In the middle of our annual routine, strangers came to do what we were doing. When conversation started, we discovered that we had common ground and history between us. Interesting, isn't it? In the midst of a cemetery we found life through the spoken word between "strangers."

The next stop on our pilgrimage was similar to the first, except for one thing. There was no church nearby, only fields and forests and a couple of farms along the road. I've always liked the setting. It's quiet, peaceful, small, and the grounds are well kept. Here as in the first stop, names and stories went with each marker to remember and talk about. Then we planted the flowers.

This pilgrimage gives us a yearly chance to visit places from our past and celebrate the lives of our loved ones. At the same time, this visit gives us time to add some beauty to their resting place as they gave us beauty during their lives with us.

Strange as it may seem, I have never found cemeteries to be depressing places or symbols only of death. Over the past few years I have found them to be a place where the promise of life becomes real. It is in this place that I have begun to question the cliché: *You only live once.*

That statement isn't entirely true, at least not for Christians. Yes, we live here on earth but once. But life isn't over with when death comes. There is life again, a new and different life. Is it a better life in a better place? I wonder about that. God made this world where we live and declared it good. And God also makes our new life in a new place with Him and declares that good too.

If the statement "you only live once" is the only truth, then maybe all the heartache we experience is only to be expected. So much of the time we desperately try to grab all the gusto we can from life, not giving much thought to someone else's dreams and hopes. Who wants to live an empty life at the expense of looking out for someone else?

But if that cliché is not entirely true, especially for Christians, then the life we live now takes on a new and different perspective. We don't have to grab and hoard things that we think might satisfy the hunger within us for a fulfilled life. Because more life is yet to come, we can truly begin to live here and now as God would have us live. There is always more and there is always a new tomorrow.

What might that new tomorrow or new life be like? Whatever it is, it will be a surprise. You and I will find life through the spoken word of God's promises. We will find life as we share our lives with others in word and deed.

Other things and activities about our yearly pilgrimage to the cemetery are cherished and memorable. But for now, it is enough to know that in that place, a place that sometimes seems empty of life, the promise of life is always present.

The promise is given in 1 Thessalonians 4:14, *"For since we believe that Jesus died and rose again, even so, through Jesus, God will bring with Him those who have died."*

23

JUNE

Is it possible for a song to bring about clarity and peace to a busy life? I think so. Has it ever seemed to you that life simply gets busier all the time? With all the technology and labor-saving devices on the market, one would think we'd have time to slow down, relax, enjoy time and leisure with family and friends more and more. So why doesn't it feel that way? About thirty years ago, I visited with a family counselor about the stresses and strains of what we called back then, *hectic lives and schedules*. She commented that we no longer led hectic lives, and she went on to say, "We now live frenzied lives." I was surprised.

The more I visit with people and the older I get, I wonder if we haven't surpassed frenzied and are onto something even more frenetically frenzied. Well, maybe that's overstating it a bit. Yet I wonder…while I will always believe that the world is good because God created it, and that there is always hope for this world and created order, because God hasn't abandoned us for messing it up through sin, life still gets a bit overwhelming and complicated at times.

This is the point in this conversation that the original question about music and song comes in, "Is it possible for a song to bring about clarity and peace to a busy life?" To which I answer, "Yes." I heard the music this last Sunday sung by a member of the church. It is an old spiritual titled "Give Me Jesus." The arrangement was simple, yet beautiful and melodic. The words were equally simple and profoundly peaceful, calming, and comforting. One musical phrase stands out from the rest: "You can have all world, just give me Jesus."

It occurred to me while I listened: that particular phrase summed up so much of what seems to be amiss in our world, while at the same time giving an answer to that dilemma. "The world" promises so much in the way of fulfillment, satisfaction, peace, purpose, contentment, and the like. Yet, "the world" is not able to deliver the goods very well. Why? There may be many reasons, but one good reason is that we don't always look in the right places or to the right people in "the world" for that which our souls, hearts, and lives long for.

That answer may sound oversimplified, and it may be—but it is a good answer. When you give that answer some time to sink in, and then ponder its significance for a while (I'm thinking a loooong while, years perhaps), there is much truth in it. The world around us tempts us to fill our lives with so much stuff, much of which is rather superfluous, though it takes wisdom to know the difference. Still, the words, "Just give me Jesus," carry within them the power of words inspired by the Holy Spirit. Let these words become a part of you each day and see where God leads you by the Spirit for the sake of His Son.

Have a great summer.

24

SEPTEMBER – OCTOBER

When I look to the gently rolling hills of west-central Minnesota, what do I see? I see a quiet beauty that stills and soothes the soul. As I gaze over the vast vista of hills and prairies, it reminds me of a dimpled quilt blanketing the prairie with warmth and beauty. I imagine soon that the trees on these hillsides will be splashed with color and texture as if painted by a divine master painter for all to enjoy. I wonder what words can describe the timeless, ageless wonder and beauty of stately trees reaching towards the heavens, awash in deep-crimson red, blazing orange, apple red, and a yellow that outshines the sun? God paints a magnificent collage for the eyes to delight in, and causes the heart to swell with wonder and gratitude for such a miracle.

Nature is nothing less than a miracle. The years sculpture the hills, the prairies, the trees, and flowers, sending us searching for words that satisfy the longings of our souls, spirits, and words that fulfill our innermost sighs.

Words and time, they go together. I wonder about the time it has taken for the hills, trees, valleys, rivers and brooks to reflect the beauty that is theirs. I wonder, and then I see our fast-paced world. Fast food, fast computers, speed limits in name only, everything moving quickly.

The Bible says that it took God seven days to create the earth, heavens, and all that is in them. If it took God seven days, why are we in such a hurry? But time is not the only fast "thing" in our world, so are words. Ever try to read a billboard with the flashing lights as you buzz by? We want words to be fast too, words of the speaker, and words of decision, judgment, and promise, and *we want them now*. I wonder if perhaps words are like the hills, trees, valleys, and creeks. It takes time to create words of beauty, meaning, and value.

I read in the Bible that God has been using the same words from the beginning (a long time, now) that He loves us, chooses us, blesses us, and saves us. Will we hear the beauty of these words as we see the beauty of the creation around us? I guess it takes time, so why do we demand instant words, instant judgment, and instant satisfaction? God has time for words to form, develop, mature, grow, and blossom into beauty.

Time and words—allowing time to let words age and mature, the more beautiful they become, making our lives richer, fuller, satisfying, and fulfilling. Aren't the best things in life worth waiting for?

I wonder if our world, including you and me and all who are reading this, will ever be able to slow down enough to hear and see the messages that God gives to us through His creation. Maybe someday, but until then, we can ask for God's help and hear His beautiful and timeless words again from the mouth of Jesus to Nicodemus, "For God so loved the world that He gave His only Son…" (John 3:16). For Jesus' sake, you are God's chosen one, forgiven and loved. You belong to God. Enjoy God's timeless beauty and timeless love.

25
JANUARY

If it hasn't already happened in your home, it will soon. The decorations from Christmas will come down, and the memories of gathered families, dinners, presents, tinsel, trees and carols will slowly become like warm embers in the fire, reminding us of the days of celebration and goodwill. In its place, the responsibilities and a more "normal" daily routine will return to our busy lives.

It is also the time that most people begin to look forward to the New Year, with a new sense of ambition and resolve to improve themselves in a variety of ways. The topic of New Year's Resolutions takes on a life of its own. As much as these resolutions are usually welcome and are actually necessary for our good, wouldn't it be nice if we could once in a while get someone else to do them for us? No, I suppose that doesn't really work, does it? Each of us has to make resolutions for ourselves, and then do or don't follow through. One good thing about resolutions is that they can be traits, habits, goals, etc. that you are already successful at and wish to improve. They can also be ones you'd like to start. There are so many resolutions to choose from that it's overwhelming. We could choose resolutions for work, marriage/relationships, family, recreation, and a host of other areas of life.

Resolutions also help us keep our priorities in line with our beliefs. With this thought in mind, I will share a few resolutions about my faith and work. I'll work on the other resolutions with my family. I'd like to resolve that I will continue to:

- Study, read, meditate, and seek understanding of God's Word.
- Be in prayer regularly.
- Give thanks to God for all the members of our parish and our worship and fellowship together.
- Faithfully preach God's Word and live it by example.
- Lead worship in a "worshipful" manner.
- Visit the sick, lonely, those who are celebrating life, and those who are dying.
- Teach God's Word and the foundations of our faith in a faithful and trustworthy manner.
- Ask for God's help and guidance in all these resolutions.

As we all face a new year with new opportunities, new possibilities, and new challenges, let us look first to God for help, guidance, direction, and perhaps mostly for forgiveness. Being human also means that in all likelihood, we will fall short of our expectations. We will need forgiveness. Only with God's help can we hope to follow through with our faith resolutions. We need God to be the foundation and source of our faith to help us through all of life's paths.

Have you thought about your resolutions yet? What might they be? Might God be part of them? There is no limit to what resolutions can be. As you consider your resolutions for the coming year, be sure to ask for God's help and guidance. You will not be sorry, and who knows, your resolutions may surprise you.

26

SEPTEMBER

It's that time of year again. Soon the halls of the schools will be ringing with the sounds of children anticipating a new school year with friends and perhaps new friends as well. Now they rush to get to their classes.

Think back to the days when you heard the song "School Days." Remember that one? It was sung nearly every day, especially by parents as they carted their little charges off to school. "School days, school days, dear old golden rule days. 'Readin' and 'ritin' and 'rithmetic'... ." That's about as far as most people got with the song. There is more but I am guessing that most are not familiar with the rest of the words.

But the song and the words certainly helped to get us in the spirit and mood for school, with all that 'readin', 'ritin,' and 'rithmetic.' The three quintessential "R's" make up the basic foundation for nearly all our learning and educational needs.

Do you suppose there are similar "R" words for our spiritual lives in anticipation of learning more about our faith? As we begin another year of confirmation instruction and Bible study, are there any basic words to describe what is foundational for our faith?

How about these for starters, "Repent, Rejoice and Respond"? With a little artistic freedom, it can be sung to the tune that we are used to…

> God's Days, God's Days
> Dear old grace-filled God's days.
> Repentin', rejoicin', respo-ondin'
> Sung to "A mighty For – or – tress….

I think we'll stop there with this verse and song and let you finish the words if you feel so moved and creative. With these three words, we have a good start on something good and useful.

When Jesus began His ministry, He preached that all should "repent' for the kingdom of heaven is near" (Matthew 4:17). Every day we need to set out anew on our journey and path of faith and life. Every day we need to ask God to cleanse us from sin, for we sin every day and need to hear His promise of forgiveness.

After receiving the gift of forgiveness, we then can rejoice for all of God's blessings.

St. Paul reminds us of this in Philippians 4:4, "Rejoice in the Lord always, again I will say, rejoice." Rejoicing is a natural reaction to blessings and gifts received from someone who loves us.

Finally, because we rejoice in the forgiveness of our sins through repentance, we can respond with loving actions and deeds for others just as God has done great things for us. Jesus said this in His sermon on the mount, "You are the light of the world….In the same way, let your light shine before others, so that they may see your good works and give glory to your Father in heaven" (Matthew 5:14-16). As Christians we believe that our faith is active in love. It's how we respond to the grace and goodness of God in all things for all the world to see.

May these three "R" words *Revive* your spirits as you *Reflect* on the grace of God to *Respond* in love each and every day.

27

SEPTEMBER – OCTOBER

It's that time of year already. Someone even suggested that the air itself feels like autumn. I suppose that's true only because of the month we are heading into. As in the past, this time of year is always hard to accept. Why is it hard to accept? Perhaps because time seems to speed by us so quickly, reminding us how little we can control time's hold and effect on us.

Time is one of those subjects that I find to be quite mysterious.

Time can be both like a friend and foe all at the same time, with each quality separated by a mere breath.

Time makes it possible to enjoy the blessings, excitement, opportunities, and joys of living.

Time is also cruel when it thoughtlessly deprives us of those same experiences in the time it takes to blink an eye.

Time is like an illusion as one day can seem to take forever to get through, while the next day passes by about as quickly as molasses flows out of a jar from the freezer.

Who can live without time? How can we live with it?

Time and its passage through our lives is just weird, I think.

People speak of doing or accomplishing something in life "when they have time." People hope and plan for the time when schedules return to "normal," and they will "have time" to do what they really want to do.

Fortunately, time is considerate and offers us the fulfillment of that wish from time to time. Unfortunately, that is not always true, and time simply passes through our hands like sand in an hourglass. Time is elusive and a tease. I wonder if it wouldn't be better to suggest that we do not "have time" in the sense of possessing it and being able to manipulate it or use it to our advantage—and better to imagine that "time has us."

I am reminded of the hymn "O God, Our Help in Ages Past" and a couple of its lines; "a thousand ages in your sight are like an evening gone….Time, like an ever-rolling stream…." This hymn is a good description of time in our lives. It is also a good reminder that God, the creator of all things, is timeless. That is, God is not bound by time's restrictions or fickleness. This hymn can also remind us that because God is timeless, He can and does give us time as a gift to be received as grace. Time is a gift we receive with gratitude. With gratitude, time can take on new meaning for us, and we may even find there is more of it that fills our lives with all the blessings, excitement and joys that come with the gift of living.

May God bless you with time over and over again.

28

JULY

Remember the nursery rhyme, "Mary, Mary quite contrary, how does your garden grow?" Well, I'm not asking if you're contrary, but how is your garden growing now? Enough time has gone by since summer started that the garden should be pretty well developed.

But why is it that my gardens never look like the ones in the magazines? In the magazines the pictures of the gardens are so fantastically beautiful that my eyes start to glaze over. Everything is perfect. Everything is in the right place, the right colors, and even the rocks are in the right and perfect place.

I have to admit that my garden isn't too bad, but it will never look like the ones in magazines. Those gardens are designed to take away all the cares of stressful living. In my garden, weeds are growing everywhere and the annuals never quite get as big, full and colorful as the magazines and ads promise. Our rock garden is exactly that, more rocks than flowers that the weeds flourish in. To top off my gardening skills, I forget what sections of the garden are planted with perennials and those that are annuals, so I sometimes work up the wrong dirt and lose a few plants along the way.

And yet even with all the flaws, I am learning to care for what is mine, and reveling in its beauty. It may not make the Victory Garden show, but it is ours, and we enjoy it, and the butterflies stop on their travels through.

I wonder if we don't look at our faith in the same way sometimes. I don't know about you, but sometimes my faith just doesn't stack up to the faith I see and read about in various publications. The rocks in my garden of faith are not in the right place, the weeds grow and grow and grow, the colors are not always as bright as some promise it would be if I practiced spiritual disciplines better. Yet, with time and grace, God allows me to see the beauty of faith He has given me. It is a different faith than yours or someone else's, but that is to be expected; we are different people with different influences and life experiences.

Still there is beauty and growth. The faith that God gives grows and matures in each of us as we water and nourish it with Word, Sacraments, and worship. I am learning that I will always have weeds to contend with and other obstacles to a perfect faith, but God is with me just as God is with you as you tend your victory garden of faith. With the Spirit's help, the sin, weeds, rocks, and other obstacles are taken away or transformed into new life and new beginnings. New faith is always being planted. Someday it will be just right, but until that comes, I will thank the Lord for what He has given me this day.

Have a great and blessed time and experience tending your gardens.

29

JULY – AUGUST

I know it isn't the safest thing to do, but as I drive through our neighboring town, I like to read the sign outside the Baptist church. Sometimes it's harder to read, and I have to strain a bit to get all the words. Usually, it takes me about three trips to get capture all the words. The last few weeks the message on the sign made me stop and wonder a bit more about God—not that I don't already think about God much of the time. The sign goes something like this, "Do you have any reading planned for this summer? Could I recommend a good book for you to read? Signed, God."

It would be a pretty obvious guess as to which book God is referring to. It would be the one He wrote along with His crew of writers who scribed all the words and bound them together over the course of centuries into the book we now call The Bible. It is indeed a great book. It is the story of God's relationship with this world, the cosmos, the galaxies, the hearts and lives of so many interesting and mysterious characters who are called, changed, and transformed people getting caught by the awesomeness and love of God.

But, if I dare say so, I would not state that this book is recommended reading. I would rather state that it is required reading for all who believe that God sent His son to live and die for the sake of the world in order to save us from our sin. It is not optional reading.

If the Bible seems a bit overwhelming to read, I would suggest starting with one of the following three books 1) Genesis (the stories are great), 2) The Book of Psalms (the poetry and message are timeless, rich and meaningful, and 3) the gospel of Mark, it is easy reading, fast-paced, intriguing and has a surprise ending. Those who read it will not be sorry and will grow to treasure, cherish, and long for these words over and over again. St. Paul writes, "Let the word of Christ dwell in you richly..." (Colossians. 3:16).

But the sign at the church also inspired another thought, "What other books might God recommend for us to read?" After all, God is the source of all words. He creates all things through words. He is a master of life-giving words. Therefore, He must love stories. What other books do you think God would have us read?

Judging from the kinds of stories in the Bible, God might recommend history, poetry, mystery, novels, and even humor. What books have you read that would deepen and inform your faith so it grows and flourishes?

As a guide to choosing other books, read what St. Paul writes to the Philippians chapter 4, "Finally, beloved, whatever is true, whatever is honorable, whatever is just, whatever is pure....if there is any excellence and if there is anything worthy of praise, think about these things."

That advice can go for reading too. Choose to read that which is good, honorable, just, and true. Have a blessed summer reading.

30

NOVEMBER – DECEMBER

Tis the season…we will soon be hearing more of that phrase in the next few weeks. However, there are days when I wonder exactly what season it really is. I mention this because recently we went out to eat at a nice, enjoyable restaurant that had a number of T.V. screens mounted on various walls. From where I sat, I was able to watch football, baseball, and women's basketball all at the same time.

I do not claim to be sports savvy. I consider myself adept at identifying the Vikings and Packers without too much confusion (they're football teams, right?), but I found it rather odd that all three were still being played. I didn't realize that these particular sports seasons overlapped so much. As I write this, I believe that the World Series hasn't even started (but will be soon), and football is well into its own season. I wondered how many other sports seasons overlap each other. For some unknown reason, I sort of figured that each sport had its own distinctive season that didn't impinge on someone else's season. I guess I figured wrong!

As I pondered this reality at the restaurant, I realized that this might be why it's difficult at times to know exactly what season we are in, about to be in, or are at the point of leaving when it comes to holidays. I go into a store in August and I see ghouls, goblins, costumes, pumpkins, turkeys, Christmas trees, lights, and even Santa Claus with all the trimmings. So what season am I really in from August on? I suppose if I just wait to see which decorations leave first that must be the season I was just in, but then it's too late to celebrate, in case I picked the wrong holiday to celebrate.

It also occurred to me that this is the November – December newsletter. We will have just finished Halloween and then All Saints Day quickly followed, with Thanksgiving and Christmas yet to come. Unless the hearts come out early for Valentine's Day, we'll have a fifty/fifty chance of getting the right season with the right holiday at the right time.

Is there a way to get it right so that when we hear the phrase "tis the season," we'll know for sure which season we are talking about?

This may seem silly, but I will also hear at various times of the year that "Jesus is the reason for the season." But which season? I believe that phrase is true, but does it come close to implying that perhaps Jesus isn't the reason for some other season? Think about that for a while.

It is true that Jesus is the main reason for our Christmas season and celebration—but it's also true that Jesus is the reason for Easter celebrations. As Christians, people of God, we can also celebrate Jesus in Valentine's Day, Memorial Day, July 4th, Labor Day, and a few of the other national yearly holidays.

Jesus is always a reason for any season. "Tis the season"….for what? Tis the season for giving thanks, remembering the blessings of family, friends, good communities, a good nation, freedoms, work, recreation, arts, music, history, memories etc., etc.

Whatever season it is, and some have more color, festivity, and activity than others, may the seasons be a blessing for you. May Jesus be your reason for every season, for Jesus is in every season for you and for me.

31

NOVEMBER

I have heard the below verse and quotation a few times recently. It is a true statement, and one that we should pay heed to lest we live out its truth.

"If a house is divided against itself, that house will not be able to stand" (Mark 3:25).

Abraham Lincoln quoted this a little differently, saying, "A house divided against itself cannot stand."

Yet I wonder exactly what "a house divided" means in relation to being able to stand or not. Does that mean that there no differences, no disagreements, and only conformity?

Let me tell you a story. There is a town, it could be any town, anywhere, but it is very small. The streets are not paved, and no curb and gutters line the streets. On some corners, the grass and weeds stand tall, hiding what trash and garbage may have been left when the tenets departed years before. Few stores exist in the downtown main street district, except for a bank, a recently closed restaurant, a couple boarded-up stores, and a grocery store that needs a new paint job and the front door needs straightening. Across the street is the old town hall with its Quonset-style architecture and wood floor, where many community events still take place.

At the north end of town is a hill where the school used to be. About a block away stands an old church. The only visible sign that it's a church are the clouded and dirty stained-glass windows. About two blocks away is another church with a tall steeple, and an old box spring mattress leaning against an outside wall.

From all outward appearances, the town is nearly deserted, except about 100 people and their pets living in small houses north and south of the railroad tracks. They've lost their school, two churches, and a few businesses. They don't want to lose anymore. In listening to conversations over coffee and lunch, one might wonder if they can stay together without losing everything. The conversations get heated; people argue and complain about each other; there seems to be more bosses than workers.

"The house" seems to be divided, and yet when it comes time to rally together, they do it well and strong. Over the years they have planned successful July 4th celebrations that rival larger towns, they have planned and held successful Seventeenth of May celebrations honoring their Norwegian heritage, attended by nearly a hundred or more people.

Why hasn't "the house" fallen? Despite their differences and even quarrels, they answer to a call greater than themselves. They look beyond themselves and see something of greater priority and importance in their lives together. You see, there is another church in town that has not closed its doors, and it has grown some, if not in numbers, then in spirit. This church is what keeps the town together because people do not want to lose another symbol of community life and vitality.

Is it true then that a house divided will always fall? Not necessarily so. It will if it can't see beyond itself and its own needs. Even if the house is divided, it can stand strong if it answers to a call and unites and commits itself to something or better yet, someone greater than itself.

God calls His people to gather as the Body of Christ in the world to witness to the truth that He is our Savior and Lord.

We are called by God to give witness to the world that we will feed the hungry, care for the lonely, the orphan, the dying, the weary, the sick, and those whose hearts are bitter. We are called to share the good news that God is active in our world and is with us each and every day.

We belong to the house and family of God, and though we may be divided, we need not fall, for God binds us together and invites us to a calling greater than ourselves.

32

JUNE

What were they to do now? Their friend, teacher, and Savior had died, then rose from the dead, and later appeared to them a number of times. It was a lot to take in, and try to make sense of. To top it all off, He left them. It was a rather spectacular departure, to say the least. As Jesus spoke His final words to His disciples, He was carried up into heaven (Luke 24:51). Perhaps as they left the hilltop where He departed from, they remembered His words to "stay in the city until you have been clothed with power from on high." And they did. They went back to the city, and as Luke writes, "they were continually in the temple blessing God" (Luke 24:53). The book of Acts also states a similar action. After returning to Jerusalem, "they entered the room upstairs where they were staying…constantly devoting themselves to prayer" (Acts 1:13-14).

What were they to do now? They were to wait until the right time was at hand. They were to wait until God acted and sent the Holy Spirit upon them. Luke writes this command in Acts 1: 4, "(Jesus) ordered them not to leave Jerusalem, but to wait there for the promise of the Father." And while they waited, they prayed and worshiped together. They prayed and worshiped because Jesus prayed and worshiped. They prayed and worshiped together because that was what they needed to do. They prayed and worshiped together because they trusted and believed that Jesus and His Father were true to their words.

God would send His Spirit and give them power and ability to be His witnesses "in Jerusalem, Judea, Samaria, and to all the ends of the earth" (Acts 1:8). But first they had to wait.

The disciples did what they had to do. Do you suppose it was hard? Do you suppose they wanted to get the show on the road and not waste precious time? After all, there were people to preach to, a story to tell, things to do, and action was needed now. But they did what Jesus ordered them to do. God would be true to His word.

Waiting is sometimes hard. It seems the human capacity for waiting and patience has grown shorter or thinner over the past decades. Try being silent, quiet, or non-active for maybe one or two complete minutes and see how long it seems. But waiting is useful and beneficial, not only to our lives but our faith as well. Luke/Acts doesn't go into much detail or explanation of why waiting is important, but it is because the disciples did, and they were blessed because of it. It was a sign of faith and trust in the words and presence of Jesus.

Perhaps we too can learn a lesson from their waiting. Perhaps the church today needs to hear this same command. Many ask, "What are we to do now?" Perhaps the thing we need to do is wait. In our waiting, we can pray and worship together, specifically and intentionally asking God for guidance, wisdom, forgiveness, and a deeper love for one another. Waiting is hard—but at times, waiting is also a sign of faith that God is indeed with us always and that God is in control, God is still Lord and King over all creation, even the church.

We'll see you in church, just like the disciples, as they were continually in the temple worshiping and praising God, waiting and watching.

33

JULY – AUGUST

I guess it's that season again, and I am reminded of the song, "Tis the season to be …." Only, this time around, it isn't the season for little white flakes falling from the sky. No, it is the season to be weeding. Actually, when you stop to think about it, isn't weeding a blessing in disguise? Would you rather be weeding in your parka? Or perhaps instead of weeding you'd like to chase piles of snow around your sidewalk with a shovel? I suppose that's a ridiculous way of looking at it, but it does put the whole task of weeding into perspective, doesn't it?

I say that because the other evening, one of those long, sort of comfortably warm evenings, I spent sitting in shorts and a t-shirt in my rock garden, pulling out many of the weeds that are gleefully and profusely reproducing themselves. In other words, my task isn't finished yet, but it's a start. While I was sitting there carefully attempting to pull each one, complete with roots, the thought crossed my mind, "Why am I doing this the hard way?" It would have been so much easier to simply get out the sprayer, fill it with water and mix up a strong dose of weed annihilator, or better yet, just spray the bottled concentrate on the weeds. On second thought, that might be a bit drastic and harmful to the flowers I am coaxing to survive. Anyway, weeding the quick way would give me more time to do more enjoyable things, right? Well…over the years, I have learned that doing things the "quick" way with "efficient" and "labor-saving" devices doesn't always deliver the "abundant time" promised. It usually just gives me more time to work at all the other jobs I haven't done yet.

In the end, I decided to stick with sitting there pulling out by hand every weed that I could at the moment. I know that in short order I will have to do it all over, provided I finish the rest of the garden I haven't even started on. The blessing in pulling weeds is that it slows me down. I can see up close the flowers that are growing. I can see others mowing, gardening and maybe weeding as well. I can hear the sounds of the community and the neighborhood, and yes, even the sound of cars on the highway. While I'm weeding, I can envision a beautiful yard or something new to try at work. I can remember the people who need remembering, and offer a prayer for them while I weed.

When you stop to think about it, there really is a lesson about life and living in weeding a garden by hand. There is a blessing in the act of weeding. If it weren't for weeds and if our gardens were always perfect, would we ever slow down to clean them out and sit and actually appreciate their beauty? The saying goes, "God works in mysterious ways," and that is certainly true with the blessings that God bestows on us in the act of weeding.

34

JANUARY

Standing, as we do every year, on the threshold of another new year, we look ahead. Almost as though straining our eyes, we long to look deep into the New Year to catch a glimpse of what might be waiting out there and up ahead for us. What is it that we see? Do we see a struggling and sagging economy offering up only a glimmer of hope for recovery, with jobs again bringing peace and stability for families? Perhaps others see a bright future filled with optimism and opportunity. For others there is the prayer that their loved ones will return safely from tours of military duty in harm's way overseas. Still, others hope, dream, long for, and pray for peace in their homes, their lives, and even for the world. What do you see?

And what do you see for the church? What do you suppose the New Year will bring for us here in our local churches as well as the larger church in society? This past year has brought the church many changes, questions to wrestle with, doubts that eat away at our spirits, and for others, a welcome change to celebrate.

For some it may seem the church is adrift on a sea where waves threaten to swamp the boat, and others may see the waves bringing us closer to God. Whether the future is something to fear or to celebrate, one thing is necessary for all—*and that is to keep our eyes on God.* For the people of God looking ahead to tomorrow, it is necessary to keep focused on Jesus. He is our light in the dark, and His word is the light to our path. He is the one we trust to lead and guide us in the ways of God.

How can you and I keep focused on Jesus and God's Word? Three habits will help. These habits are not easy, and they are not the only habits needed, but they are a beginning. 1) Read God's Word, 2) Pray, and 3) Worship. When these habits are difficult to begin or maintain, the Holy Spirit will lead us, call us and give us the faith and ability to continue. Through these habits, the Spirit will nurture and cause our faith to grow so that we become what God desires us to be: believers of His Word.

As for the New Year, I wish I knew what this New Year held in store for you, me, the church, and maybe even the world, but I don't know for certain. However, I do know who holds the church and the New Year, and it is God. Only with God's help can I keep my eyes of faith on Him. With God, you and I can go into the future knowing that we are not alone, and God promises to be with us until the end of the age.

35

DECEMBER

I write this before Christmas, looking out my office window upon a world covered with a new blanket of snow. It is a beautiful sight. For a while, the world's flaws, shortcomings, and uncertainties are covered. Their presence is only acknowledged by their forms outlined by the newly fallen snow. Certainly, the Christmas season is the better for such beauty and peace that comes with fresh snow. By the time you read this, the Christmas tree will be packed away or thrown out onto the curb, and the decorations, wrapping paper; ribbons and bows will be put away for yet another year. The season of color, festivities, feasts, family gatherings, and presents will be fading as the routines of life, work, and responsibilities return.

Is there a way to keep the "spirit" of Christmas alive and bright? Yes, there is. It is in telling the story again and again of why we celebrate. It is in telling the story of why we gather as families. It is in telling the story of why we give gifts of love to another. It is in telling the story of why we celebrate the birth of Jesus, the Savior. Regardless of what the world might want to make of Christmas or the holiday season, the reason we celebrate it as we do and have for centuries with all the added features of music, trees, gifts, and color is because of Jesus.

How do I know that telling the stories, again and again, will keep the "spirit" of Christmas alive and well? My wife tells the story that she remembers her first birthday. She remembers carrying cupcakes to give the students in her mother's high school English class celebrating that festive day. She doesn't remember other birthdays, perhaps at least until ages 6 or 7, because those weren't as spectacular, and no one told her those stories.

If carrying cupcakes is worthy of telling again and again, so is the story of Jesus' birth.

Tell the story of the reason you celebrate and give thanks to God for all the blessings and gifts He has given to you.

Tell the story of the Love of God that transforms the world and changes people's hearts and lives.

Tell the story so that generations to come and "people yet unborn may praise the Lord….so that the name of the Lord may be declared….when peoples gather together to worship the Lord" (Psalm 102: 18, 21, 22).

The spirit, joy, and festivities of Christmas aren't just for the cold, snowy winter months but are true the whole year around. Tell the story by keeping one nativity scene out the whole year in your home. When we tell the story either in word or deed, the words of St. Paul ring true, "But how are they to call on one in whom they have not believed? And how are they to believe in one of whom they have never heard? And how are they to hear without someone to proclaim him?" (Romans 10:14).

May the reason and God's spirit of Christmas be with you in every season as the New Year begins to unfold before you.

36

DECEMBER

We have entered that time of year known as "the holiday season." It is a mixture of Thanksgiving, Advent, and Christmas all rolled into one. It's hard to tell exactly when one season ends, and another begins. Actually, it should be obvious which season it is since each has their own symbol or person associated with it. Turkeys are for Thanksgiving. Mary, Joseph, Jesus, the shepherds, and the Wisemen are for Christmas, as is Santa Claus (history shows us he's another religious figure that has evolved through history into a secular icon). Occasionally, a turkey is fitted out in a Santa outfit and thus, the two seasons are blended.

Thankfully, Thanksgiving has not yet been as over-commercialized as other holidays, so we were able to celebrate that one more or less as it was intended. Christmas is such a big seller and becomes so commercial that we miss out on Advent, except in church, of course. Even there, it's difficult to celebrate Advent for what it is meant to signify. What is Advent? Advent is a time of preparation and anticipation. It is a time of waiting expectantly for something to happen. Liturgically speaking, it means to sing Advent carols and not Christmas carols, it means to not put up the Nativity scene too soon, and certainly not to put out baby Jesus until Christmas Eve. Is this what we do? No. Is this what I do at home? No. Is this what we should do in church?

Waiting is hard. It's become even more difficult in recent years with the type of schedules, plans, work, and expectations we've come to live with and regard as normal. Who wants to wait for anything? As I saw on a t-shirt recently, "Instant gratification is too slow!"

But that is what we are called to do. Wait and prepare for the Savior. However, it isn't just a "sit and wait" or a "waiting without purpose" or a "mindless and boring waiting" that we are called to engage in. It is an "exciting and anticipatory waiting." We wait with "bated breath" for the promise of God to come true. We wait with an eagerness that causes us to be on our toes with joy, and excitement in our eyes because we know that something great is about to happen. The waiting and preparations we engage in would be like the waiting that families do for a baby about to be born, or a loved one to come home after a long absence. But in the waiting, there is preparation. Meals are planned, activities are planned, housecleaning is done, and a host of other tasks, chores, and projects are finished so that everything is just right when the grand and big moment arrives.

This is Advent. This is the season we are in. Advent is the time to prepare our hearts and lives for the coming Messiah, the fulfillment of God's promises for the world, for you and me. Advent is a time filled with blessings if we are patient to see them and seek to be faithful to the intent and meaning of Advent. Now is the time to prepare your heart and life with God's Word, prayer, praise, and worship, so that when the day comes, and we celebrate the good news of Jesus' birth, we will be ready as we can possibly be. Advent is the season to wait expectantly and with grace-filled joyous anticipation that borders on a jovial and bubbly excitement that can hardly contain itself for the birth of Jesus to arrive. Until then, let's wait.

37

DECEMBER

It's in the eyes. That is how one can tell.

Once I was visiting with some brothers while they sat with their aged mother in a nursing home room. At first glance, they did not look at all alike, but as we sat and conversed, the resemblance became clearer. One was sitting by the bedside of his mother who was very ill. His brother sat in a chair not too far away. As the one talked, he would look at his mother and then at his brother and me during our visit. As he did so, I remembered what his mother looked like when she was not so ill. I remembered her face and her eyes. As her son held her hand, his eyes gave his thoughts and feelings away. As the three of us sat in that place conversing and watching life ebb and flow in the woman in the bed, it was the eyes of the brothers that connected them to each other and their mother. Their eyes were the windows to their souls.

Looking into a person's eyes is risky business. It is risky because much of who we are, if not everything we are, is reflected in our eyes. Haven't you ever been fearful to look someone in the eye? Some have a dark, penetrating look that invades and unsettles. At the same time, others have troubled, restless eyes that never stop moving. Then there are the eyes of grace and love—eyes that seem to envelop and surround one with graciousness and life.

It's in the eyes. In this time that we await the birth of our Savior, I have often wondered why God chose to live among us beginning as a baby. The Infinite God, Eternal Being, Light of Light, and God of gods, shrouded in spirit and mystery, became a baby, the man Jesus. He took on flesh and blood and He had eyes. He had eyes to reflect the life within him.

It's risky business to look into the eyes of Jesus, for who will we see? Will we see the baby in Bethlehem, soft and innocent, or a young man of 12 questioning His teachers in the Temple? Will we see a grown man calling His disciples to repentance and discipleship? Will we find His gaze penetrating and unsettling or comforting and gracious? It's risky business to look into the eyes of a man who on the cross prays that His father/God would forgive those who put Him there, while He himself forgives the repentant thief on another cross.

Why is it risky? Because in Jesus' eyes, we see the Father, the God who created the heavens and the earth. We see in the eyes of Jesus the God who so loved the world that He gave His only son to live and die that His world might be saved and have life. In Jesus' eyes, we see the relationship and connection between a Father and a Son. The eyes of Jesus are indeed the window to His spirit, the spirit of love, forgiveness, mercy, kindness, faithfulness, and gentleness that He receives from His Father.

In this blessed Advent and Christmas season, may you see Him not only with new eyes but also see Him in the eyes of all you meet.

38

AUGUST

There are days and even weeks when it seems nothing goes right. One might even wonder, "What's God up to in my life? Why is all this stuff happening? Is He trying to teach me something?" You've heard the phrase, "When it rains, it pours." That may be good when it's actually rain that falls. When it seems that mishaps, misunderstandings, miscommunications, and other varied "accidents" of life occur in rapid succession, it makes one wonder where, if, and how God is involved in all this.

At least I wonder because some of that happened at our home recently. It's nothing real serious. Our washing machine, water heater, water dispenser on the refrigerator, water softener and two cars start going on the blink all about the same time. With the subsequent bills about to arrive, I start to wonder if either Satan is out to get me or if God is trying to teach me something about life. I wondered, maybe both possibilities are true. Maybe Satan is working overtime to distract me from trusting God to provide and care for me, while God is indeed working in those mishaps to teach me trust and faith. A verse from Romans 8 comes to mind: "We know that in all things God works for good for those who love Him and are called according to His purpose" (v. 28, translation from other ancient sources listed as a footnote in the New Revised Standard Version).

That verse provided a source of good news for the latest mishap with our vehicles. The engine belt fell off while pulling the watering trailer in the morning, and we had to go to plan

"B." After a bit of frustration and irritation, it became clear to me that the "mishap" happened at the right time. If it had happened about an hour later, my wife would have been stranded somewhere between home and Minneapolis. I believe that God was "in" that mishap working something out for good. It sounds a bit trite, but there is a lesson in this.

The lesson is that God is indeed in all things working out His will and something good. God is in the midst of what looks and feels like chaos, disorder, darkness, and even death, and He is working out His will and creating order and light. It started with Genesis and continues on through Revelation and into eternity. Bad things happen; Satan is working to create disorder, chaos, and darkness. But God is greater, and God is in the midst of all things.

In the life of the Church—the body of Christ, universal—there are bad things that happen, mistakes made, bad decisions, good decisions, good achievements, and even confusing things. Such is the state of the Church today. People wonder, and I wonder, and wrestle with how to be faithful and true to God and Scripture and the faith as it has been handed down to me and entrusted to me as a pastor. Some days are better than others, but through it all day by day, I am convinced of the promise in St. Paul's words in Romans 8, "We know that in all things God works for good for those who love Him and are called according to His purpose." God is with us in our congregations, our parish and the whole Church (Lutheran, Baptist, Methodist, Charismatic, Catholic, Presbyterian, Assembly of God, etc. etc.) working for good and His purposes.

Something good will happen, someday, somehow, but only by God's hand. Let us keep our eyes, ears, and hearts focused on God's Word and God's promises that He is with us in all things every day.

39

JANUARY

The afterglow of Christmas is a time that is ripe for some rather melancholic thoughts and feelings. The excitement and buildup of get-togethers, food, presents, color, light, and decorations is nearly over, and we can slow up again and get back to "normal."

It's okay to take some time and ponder the events of the past few weeks. It's okay to come down from all the excitement, colors, packaging, music, tinsel, and more that this season holds. It's okay because life is like that. It's good to have the excitement, and it's good to be quiet and full of deep thoughts, and heartfelt ponderings. These all make the season even more meaningful. The meaning of Christmas is one that changed the world, and it changes lives. The afterglow doesn't have to mean that the light and excitement are completely over or extinguished. The afterglow is merely the reminder that the embers of what happened at Christmas is still warm, relevant, and real. Let us pray that we can keep the embers, the afterglow burning for a long time.

How can we do that? It really isn't as hard as it seems. Like a fire in the fireplace, when there are embers all one has to do is occasionally put a log on, and the fire continues to burn brightly and warmly. With our hearts, especially in regards to the Christian faith that is planted in our hearts, this keeping the fires going is done when we pray, when we worship, and when we read God's Word. In worship we gather together with others who have heard and seen what the angels announced so brilliantly. In worship we continue to hear the good news from God's Word that is given for all to hear, "that to you is born a Savior" and this Savior comes each and every day and week to give you His promises of peace, forgiveness, mercy, and love, to name but a few. In your homes, you can continue to pray with praise and thanksgiving for all that God has done. In your quiet moments, you too, like Mary, can treasure all the stories of what God has done for you and ponder them in your heart.

To keep the embers and afterglow alive, I wouldn't bother much with New Year's resolutions. At least not the kind we usually make because they don't last very long, and most likely cause unhealthy guilt. Perhaps in the afterglow of Christmas, we can pray that God will simply use us as instruments of the peace that He gives to us in Jesus. Perhaps we can pray that the peace of God and His son Jesus will flow through us and become real in the lives of others. It involves merely sharing the gift that is given to us from above. We don't have to manufacture that peace; we don't have to work up enough sincerity to share it. We simply have to ask God to help us give what He has already given us, and then let the Spirit do its work.

Have a blessed New Year in the afterglow of a glorious Christmas.

40

JULY – AUGUST

Recently we watched an old Disney classic movie, "Mary Poppins," a favorite around our house. In the last scene, the Banks family fly kites along with many others in their neighborhood. It is a fitting end to a marvelous story. There is something about flying kites that is exhilarating and exciting. When our son was much younger, he loved to fly kites in the meadow, as we called it, next to our house. He would come to me and ask, "Dad, is it a good day to fly a kite?" He always hoped for a positive answer so he could run and get his kite.

What is it about flying a kite that is so appealing? What is it about catching the wind in a kite, sending it heavenward that is intriguing, pleasing, and satisfying? Perhaps it is the feeling that we can fly ourselves up in the air, free like a bird. Flying a kite, though, is also a challenge. When our son was trying to get his kite in the air, sometimes he had to run and run and run, and then throw the kite into the air to catch the wind. He would ask his sister, mother, or me for help because he was certain that if we tried hard enough, it would work. When the kite did "catch the wind," it certainly was exciting to see how high and long we could keep the kite up where the birds flew, up in the heavens.

In time the phrase "go fly a kite" took on new meaning. How so? Think of it this way. In the Hebrew language, the word for "wind" is the same word for "spirit." When our son was catching the "wind" for his kite, he was so to speak also catching "the spirit" that made not only his kite fly but also his own heart, imagination, and excitement. So it is with our faith, our life together both in community and in our places of worship. How will we in our parish "catch the spirit/the wind" of God to make our kites, our hearts, souls and imaginations soar? God makes His spirit, His wind blow among us every day, every week. God is among us, His spirit is blowing in our midst. In our worship, in our times of study, in our personal devotion time, God's spirit is blowing. In our times of fellowship and work, God's spirit is blowing. How can we throw our kites up into the skies to catch that spirit, that wind, so our lives and spirits catch the excitement and thrill of flying the kites that God gives to us?

We catch the spirit when we gather for worship and fellowship, and when we work together for common goals. We catch the spirit when we make time for God in our lives through reading His word, prayer, and devotional time. Like flying a kite, we need to be persistent because it's not always easy to catch the wind/spirit. Because of sin and temptations, catching the spirit is a challenge. We need to ask others for help to come and "catch the spirit" with us, so our kites will fly.

When by God's grace we catch the spirit/wind of God, we experience the exhilaration, excitement, and satisfaction that comes with seeing our life together filled with the spirit soaring skyward. So "go fly a kite"—invite someone to worship, take on a new commitment at church or in the community, pray for the ministry that we do here, give thanks to God for our members, support the ministry and fellowship that is offered weekly, monthly and yearly. Thanks be to God who keeps sending His wind so that our kites might be filled with His Spirit.

41

AUGUST

I can hardly believe it happened. I never thought I would hear these words come from my mouth: "Let's go fishing!" The words sounded simple and innocent enough, but for someone who rarely jumped at any occasion to go fishing, no matter how promising the adventure may have been, the fact that I said these words at all is probably close to a miracle.

Except for the cost of the license, for which I intended to get good use of, I found that I actually looked forward to the adventure, and was nearly "in a rush" getting my children and me out the door. I had visions of sitting on a rock beside a quiet, babbling brook that meandered through a pastoral pasture, while white cottony clouds floated lazily above our heads in the blue eternal expanse. Oh yes, and catching fish too.

What a dream. While the dream may not have materialized precisely as I envisioned, we all had a very good time. The children enjoyed hanging onto their bamboo poles while dangling the fishing line, with the red and white bobber in the water, and eagerly waiting for the bobber to disappear and feel that "tug" in the line, a sure sign of a catch.

Sometime during the day, we had lunch, listened to the birds, and watched fish jump at insects skimming the water surface. Then we watched the sun slowly set behind the hills, marking the end of a perfectly wondrous afternoon.

Where is the miracle in all this? Perhaps it is this: what will a father do for his children so that they might enjoy one of life's adventures. I never was much of a fisherman, so I am not sure where my children attained the great desire to fish. The miracle is that just as my father took me fishing (though I don't know where he got the patience to do so) so I am taking my children fishing. What a father won't do for his children.

There really is something to this fishing activity, even with a six-year-old and a three-year-old. Fishing provides a time to simply chat, listen to each other, be lazy, watch the fish, and listen to the birds. In other words, fishing provides the makings for memories of time spent with one's father, mother, brother, sister or other loved one. The truth of fishing and living is hard to describe, but it's easy to feel.

"What a father won't do for his children". This also makes me think of God, our heavenly father. What makes God do the things He does for us, His children? It must be a miracle. It must be love.

You may be wondering if we caught any fish that day. Does it really matter?

May you also enjoy, savor, cherish and live to the fullest your times with your children—but also times with your heavenly Father.

42

JULY – AUGUST

Over the years, I have listened and watched farmers as they prepare the fields, plant the seeds, and then wait and wonder what sort of crop they might receive in the end. With this comes a bit of apprehension not knowing what sort of weather and other factors might play out as the crops grow.

It must be hard to be a farmer. As the seeds are planted, hope is also planted. Hope that the seeds sprout, that there will be favorable weather, no insects, blight, or other natural disasters to endanger the seeds and crops.

Yet seeds are sown, faith is lived out, and the farmer continues to farm. Let us thank God that the farmer lives with such faith.

Over the years, I have also noticed parents with small children. It seems most families are on the run with full schedules and daily routines. There is the usual apprehension about raising children in a world such as ours. Now with our children grown, the worries and concerns only change their size and make-up. It is not easy to raise a family.

However, parents plant the seeds of right and wrong, good values, love, and acceptance. Hope is planted too, hope that children will remain healthy and safe, grow up to make right and wise decisions about friends, careers, marriage partners, schools, etc., etc.

Parents, too, live a life of faith. Let us thank the Lord for faithful parents who continue to plant seeds of faith in their children's lives.

I have talked with pastors of large churches, small churches, and those in between. There is the usual concern about the future, about the life, vitality, and health of a congregation.

Sometimes it is hard to be a pastor. Seeds are sown, and hope is planted. Hope that the cares and worries of the world and living don't choke the life out of parishioners and their families.

Still, the seeds of faith and the Good News of Jesus are proclaimed and sown in the lives of people through worship, prayer, song, Sacraments, and ordinary daily deeds of love and concern. Let us thank the Lord that the people of God still plant seeds whenever and wherever they gather and live out their lives.

When I visit with some of our older members, I hear their concerns. It seems age and time is not always a friend. The eyes, ears, muscles, and stamina aren't quite what they used to be.

It isn't easy growing older. Friends die, life gets lonely, people are in a rush, and who has time to visit and sit a spell?

Yet seeds are planted, seeds of hope, seeds of prayer for families, friends, churches, and neighbors. Hope is planted too, hope that tomorrow someone may visit, and hope that prayers are not prayed in vain.

Let us thank the Lord for the faithful and the bit-older generations for their prayers, for the seeds of faith they have sown and continue to sow.

And then I think of God. God is like the farmer, parents and children, the pastor, and our elders. He plants seeds, and He hopes. God works so that His seeds bear fruit.

Let us thank God for being faithful. He always stands by us, sowing the good seed of His word and promises.

May your seasons of planting "seeds" be fruitful and blessed.

About the Author

Paul R. Johnson grew up in a parsonage. He received his A.A. degree in Music from Waldorf College, Forest City, Iowa, and B.A. degree in Business Administration from Concordia College, Moorhead, Minnesota, and his M. Div. degree from Luther Seminary, St. Paul, Minnesota. His ministry has spanned over 34 years to congregations in North Dakota, South Dakota, and Minnesota.

He shares his life with his multitalented spouse, and their two children. In his spare time, Paul enjoys music, especially playing the piano, hiking, camping, caning chairs, handwork, and a few other things.

www.ingramcontent.com/pod-product-compliance
Lightning Source LLC
Chambersburg PA
CBHW052114110526
44592CB00013B/1608

A hike in the woods is always an adventure of what is known an unknown. What is known may be the path itself or the certainty of beaut and peace that the woods provide. What is unknown are the surprise that one finds along the way. One day it may be a new wildflower, different songbird, or a fawn. Another day may bring new tracks o coyotes, raccoons, and other critters walking the same path.

The essays in this book are like that hike in the woods. Each piece is a adventure in the Christian faith of what is known and what is unknown What is known are the fundamental truths we cling to and claim a children and people of God. What is unknown in this adventure of faithfu living is what we will experience, feel, think, or imagine about faith durin any given month or season. Because we have the promise of God presence with us every day in this adventure, we continue on the pat anticipating a new encounter with God every day.

May your journey on this path be an adventure of discovery and faith.

It has been my privilege and pleasure to receive the regular newsletter from Pastor Paul's parish. I have found his articles to be very readable, interesting, and a blessing.

In his writing Pastor Paul is a good teacher providing some excellent lessons. He asks good questions and answers them very well. He uses humor, wit, subtlety, and everyday experience. (He shares Scripture and an occasional quote from a book.) He sets forth simple lessons and serious thoughts about life, and best of all, he shares a clear Gospel of Jesus Christ. Thanks be to God for his ministry of writing.
—Pastor Arvin Halvorson

FUZIONPRESS

$14.95
ISBN 978-1-946195-81-4